Sign up for my newsletter to receive MY Crappy
Ideas to grow a business and get this
free ebook too:

50 Ways To Have Fun At Work
Improve Employee Morale &
Hopefully Not Get Fired!

Just send an email to
crappyideas@richdigirolamo.com

Crappy Ideas: they all don't stink

If you're like most people you sit and think about things while "doing your business." Or worse....you forget all the great crap you think about after you're done crapping. This journal is designed for those times.

Crappy Ideas......is just that.......a place to dump all those gazillion dollar ideas you think about when............well.....when you're taking a crap.

Following are a few ideas that didn't get flushed away while I was doing my business on how to use this business version of **Crappy Ideas**:

1. If you have gender specific employee bathrooms you can see which sex has the better ideas by periodically switching the location of your Crappy Ideas journal (or just order a second one now and make it a contest.)
2. Write only one idea per page. This way when others pick up the book they can build on the Idea Dump of others.
3. Take your Crappy Ideas journal to staff/team/status meetings and discuss some of the entries.
4. What, you're an entrepreneur and work from home? Your family wonders what the heck it is you do all day anyway. Here's the opportunity to let them know what you're thinking/doing — and even enlist their help!
5. Don't just write! Draw your ideas! Yes, that's why there are no lines on the page, silly!

They say the best thinking happens in the shower. Shower. Toilet. Same thing. The best thinking happens when you're taking care of business! So get going.....Build and grow that business while doing your business!

they all don't stink

Crappy Ideas

they all don't stink

Crappy Ideas

they all don't stink

Crappy Ideas

they all don't stink

Crappy Ideas

they all don't stink

Crappy Ideas

they all don't stink

Crappy Ideas

they all don't stink

Crappy Ideas

they all don't stink

Crappy Ideas

they all don't stink

Crappy Ideas

they all don't stink

Crappy Ideas

they all don't stink

Crappy Ideas

they all don't stink

Crappy Ideas

they all don't stink

Crappy Ideas

they all don't stink

Crappy Ideas

they all don't stink

Crappy Ideas

they all don't stink

Crappy Ideas

they all don't stink

Crappy Ideas

they all don't stink

Crappy Ideas

they all don't stink

Crappy Ideas

they all don't stink

Crappy Ideas

they all don't stink

Crappy Ideas

they all don't stink

Crappy Ideas

they all don't stink

Crappy Ideas

they all don't stink

Crappy Ideas

they all don't stink

Crappy Ideas

they all don't stink

Crappy Ideas

they all don't stink

Crappy Ideas

they all don't stink

Crappy Ideas

they all don't stink

Crappy Ideas

they all don't stink

Crappy Ideas

they all don't stink

Crappy Ideas

they all don't stink

Crappy Ideas

they all don't stink

Crappy Ideas

they all don't stink

Crappy Ideas

they all don't stink

Crappy Ideas

they all don't stink

Crappy Ideas

they all don't stink

Crappy Ideas

they all don't stink

Crappy Ideas

they all don't stink

Crappy Ideas

they all don't stink

Crappy Ideas

they all don't stink

Crappy Ideas

they all don't stink

Crappy Ideas

they all don't stink

Crappy Ideas

they all don't stink

Crappy Ideas

they all don't stink

Crappy Ideas

they all don't stink

Crappy Ideas

they all don't stink

Crappy Ideas

they all don't stink

Crappy Ideas

they all don't stink

Crappy Ideas

they all don't stink

Crappy Ideas

they all don't stink

Crappy Ideas

they all don't stink

Crappy Ideas